WE BECAME

Written and Illustrated by
EVE FRANCIS

WestBow Press books may be ordered through booksellers or by contacting:

WestBow Press
A Division of Thomas Nelson & Zondervan
1663 Liberty Drive
Bloomington, IN 47403
www.westbowpress.com
844-714-3454

Scripture quotations taken from The Holy Bible, New International Version® NIV®
Copyright © 1973 1978 1984 2011 by Biblica, Inc. TM
Used by permission. All rights reserved worldwide.

ISBN: 978-1-6642-6717-6 (sc)
ISBN: 978-1-6642-6719-0 (hc)
ISBN: 978-1-6642-6718-3 (e)

Library of Congress Control Number: 2022909375

Print information available on the last page.

WestBow Press rev. date: 06/14/2022

WestBow
PRESS®
A DIVISION OF THOMAS NELSON
& ZONDERVAN

Read the story. Return here for a game.
Now count how many careers you can name.

WE BECAME

Written and Illustrated by
EVE FRANCIS

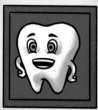

Be sure to read **Eve Francis'** prequel *"Beautifully and Wonderfully Made"*. This first story is about a little girl named Jacqueline. She is nervous about her first day of Kindergarten because she has a fluttering eye. By the end of the day, she has met eighteen other students who have some type of physical/mental challenge. Jacqueline is delighted to have made friends who are just like her who are happy, confident, and secure in who they are. Jacqueline is comforted and smiles as she learns that all children are *"Beautifully and Wonderfully Made"*.

SEEK & FIND
"No matter your size, no matter your ages, seek and
you'll find a small dove on some pages."

HOPE
"When the dove returned to him in the evening, there
in its beak was a freshly plucked olive leaf!"
Genesis 8:11 NIV

This book is dedicated to all students who overcame their inhibitions of unique challenges and became successful adults in their chosen professions.

"Trust in the LORD with all your heart, and do not lean on your own understanding. In all your ways acknowledge Him, and He will make straight your paths."
Proverbs 3:5-6 NIV

This is a story about girls and boys,

Born with some challenges turned into joys!

Blindness, cleft pallet, Down syndrome and heart,
No obstacles here. We're special and smart!

Jeremiah 29:11 NIV-"For I know the plans I have for you," declares the LORD, "plans to prosper you and not to harm you, plans to give you hope and a future."

My name is Jacqueline. I'm here to say,
My fluttering eye did not get in the way!

I did not let it become a disaster.
I chose to become a famous newscaster!

Hi there. I'm Zeke. I used to be nervous.
Now I am working in public service!
Hoses and ladders make my job lighter.
I volunteer as a firefighter!

In my regular job I dress in blue,
Protecting all people. That means you too!
My radio tells me where I need to be,
Policemen respond to emergencies!

Elizabeth here. From wheelchair to court,
My job is to type words into reports!

Recording the truth is what I prefer.
I am a typist; a court reporter!

Cole is my name and I liked to chew gum.
It helped me listen and have great outcomes!

I am successful although I won't boast,
My occupation? A radio host!

Hi! I'm Macie. I wore gold-speckled glasses.
I stood out in style in all of my classes!

My dream to become a scholastic creature.
Came true as an elementary teacher!

I'm glad to meet you. My name is Karson.
I prayed to become a sign language parson!

Answered prayer told me as a worshiper,
My call would be as a school interpreter!

I'm Angelique. I could not pay attention.
My life's career is to show comprehension!

My work is with a publishing company.
I knew one day I'd be a great somebody!

My name is Blake. I had ADHD.
I jumped in the hallway on a trampoline!

The school days were long and I cried and cried.
Delivering mail gives me freedom outside!

Hello there. I'm Ann who wore leg braces.
T'was sad that I couldn't join any races!

Childhood was sometimes a time of great stress,
'Til I found my job as a flight stewardess!

Hey there. How are you? My name is Cooper.
Despite my heart problems I'm doing super!

Medicine, patience and being persistent,
Helped me become a physician's assistant!

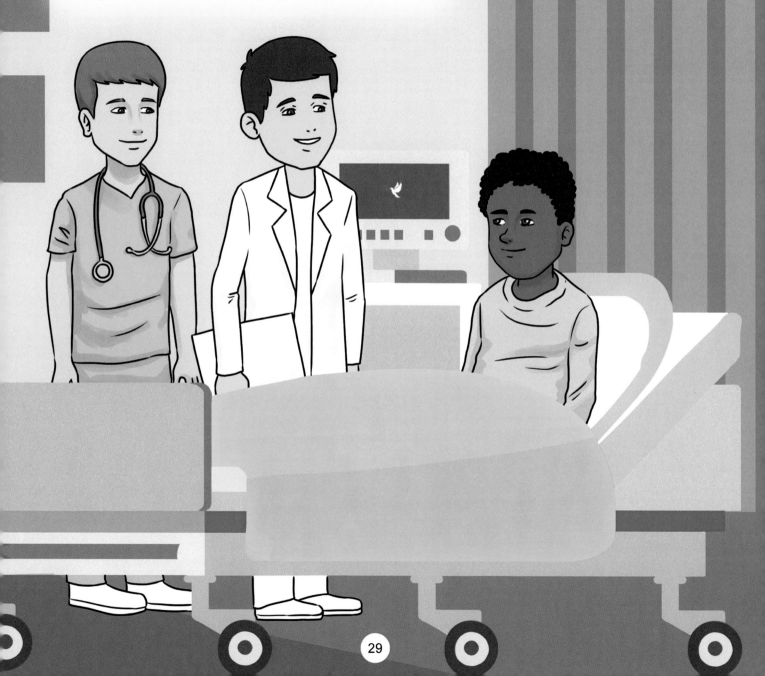

Excuse me, hello. My name's Adaline.
I wore hearing aids which helped me to shine!

Instruments and music were my ambition.
I love my job! A concert musician!

My name is Kendall which means Royal Valley.
My special smile was like a crooked alley!

Now I smile wide which I can not prevent,
I'm happy to be a dental assistant!

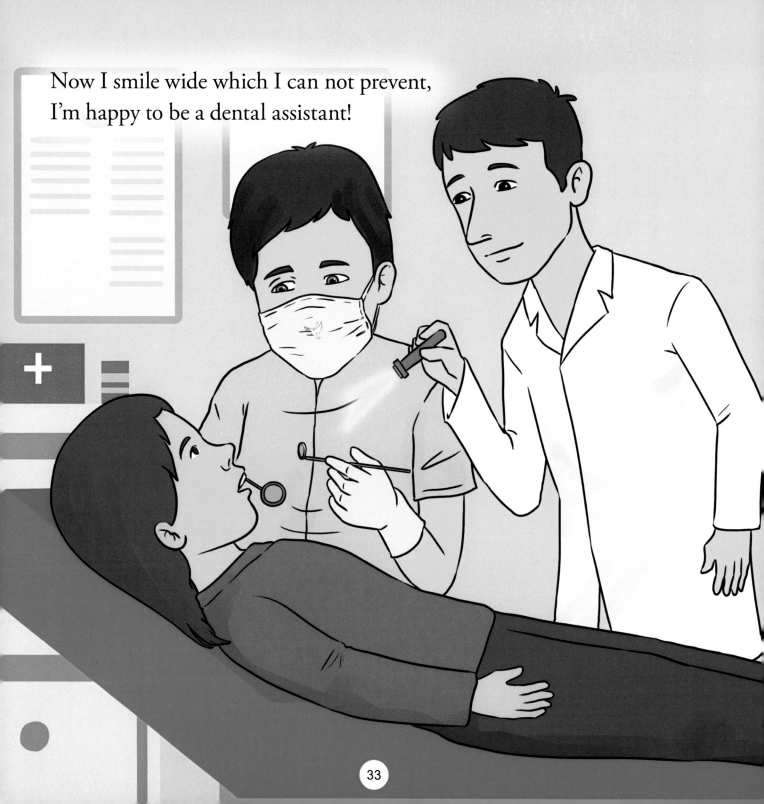

My talking box told friends my name was Paige.
Today I'm courageous to take the main stage!

Speaking all day is a major factor,
I star in plays as a leading actor!

Hi! I am Brock. I have dreams just like you.
I get all my food through a feeding tube!

My camera in hand, you take your places.
I'm a photographer who snaps your faces!

Hi! I am Claire and I am diabetic.
This hasn't stopped me from being athletic!

I've liked to help others since I was little.
I'm a nutritionist at a hospital!

I am Gideon. I liked to climb and sled.
I wore a helmet to help protect my head!

I talk to people. My boss says I'm a star,
I'm a car salesman! I help you buy a car!

Hello! I'm Quinn. I'm pleased that we could meet.
Eye contact is hard, but I will not retreat!

Because it's difficult, sometimes I rehearse.
Face to face I succeed. I am a nurse!

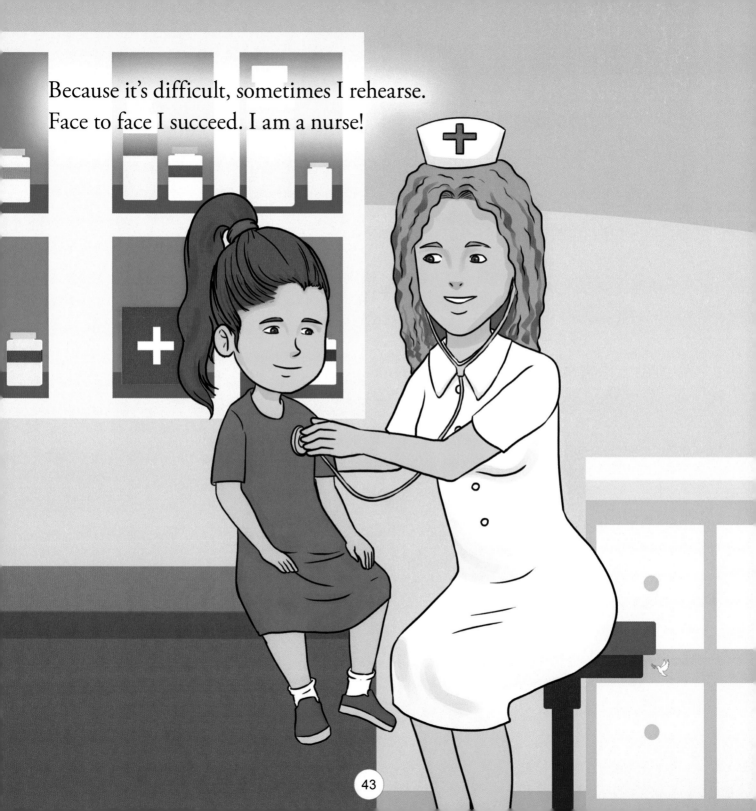

Please shake my hand. I'm Hunter and I'm blind.
My life has been great because people were kind!

Hello. I'm Chad and I didn't like to speak.
At times my words repeated and they were weak!

As different as snowflakes and blades of grass,
We are all special, unique and first-class.

No matter our challenges, no matter our name,
What is important is that *We Became*!

Jeremiah 29:11 NIV-"For I know the plans I have for you," declares the LORD, "plans to prosper you and not to harm you, plans to give you hope and a future."

Watch for the third book in the Cherub Chat series entitled *"Hooray! Namaw's House!"*

This story is about a brother and sister who spend the day with Namaw and Papa while their parents are away for the day. The reader(s) will experience the natural bond of loving fun that is shared between grandparents and grandchildren that benefits the entire family.

ABOUT THE AUTHOR EVE FRANCIS

Eve Francis loves The Lord and her family beyond measure! She is a loving and passionate wife, mother and grandmother. Eve believes that all children are a gift from God. Every single child is a reward and a blessing! All children are beautifully and wonderfully made! Eve enjoyed a lifetime career centered around children. Her experience with children began as a young girl who babysat the neighborhood children. Later in life Eve started a cherub choir (The Angelics) that she originated for children aged three through second grade. Eve also had a Christian childcare (TenderCare) in her home for children from the newborn age through age five. The forte of her employment was as a Special Educational Assistant. In her spare time, Eve is a Christian concept painter who honors God with scripture supported artwork. Once retired she blossomed into a full-time Christian published author who writes novels and children's books. Eve enjoys a rich and rewarding life with the love of her life, her husband.

You can follow Eve on her Facebook page Eve Carton Francis and write to her at Eve@CherubChat.com.